Time Management

Acquire Proficiency In Time Management Techniques And Gain Insights On Enhancing Efficiency, Optimizing Time, Structuring Your Life, And Attaining Your Objectives Immediately

ÄtheFellinger

TABLE OF CONTENT

Considerations Of Oneself 1

Teamwork Is Difficult 10

Real-World Applications Of The Pomodoro Technique 19

Real-World Applications Of The Pomodoro Technique 31

Planning And Goal-Setting Effectively: Matching Objectives With Time Allocative 37

Creating The Ideal Calendar 42

How To Beat Procrastination 46

Effective Schedule Design And Planning 54

Setting Goals And Organizing 79

Some Examples And Case Studies Of How These Principles And Strategies Have Worked For Successful People Or Organisations 86

Attaining Equilibrium Between Professional And Personal Life And Effectively Coping With Stress 100

The Fallout From Ineffective Time Management. 135

Considerations Of Oneself

Self-knowledge and Reflection

Assessing oneself is a crucial component in the process of managing time efficiently.

Prior to implementing management strategies and techniques, it is imperative to possess a comprehensive understanding of one's own skills, preferences, and behavioral patterns.

Self-awareness and introspection play a crucial role in this undertaking.

Allocate time for introspection and contemplate upon your individual priorities, values, and objectives.

This can be achieved by engaging in activities such as maintaining a personal diary, engaging in meditation practices, or seeking guidance from a mentor or a professional coach.

This self-evaluation will enable you to discern your strengths, areas for improvement, and potential avenues for personal development.

Assessment of Advantages and Limitations

Upon preliminary contemplation, it is imperative to discern one's proficiencies and deficiencies in relation to the management of time.

This will assist you in optimizing your skills and formulating effective approaches to overcome obstacles.

Examine and assess your aptitude in the areas of planning, organizing, prioritizing, concentrating, and exercising self-control.

Engage in self-reflection regarding instances wherein you experienced heightened productivity and efficiency, discerning the key aptitudes that facilitated such instances, and contemplate how you can transfer and employ them in different spheres of your life.

In a similar vein, ascertain barriers and tendencies that may impede the effective management of your time.

Potential causes for this behavior could include the tendency to delay tasks, challenges in declining requests, an absence of an organized framework, or a proclivity to become swiftly diverted.

By acknowledging these aforementioned limitations, you will be more adequately equipped to devise efficacious solutions and strategies.

Definition of Improvement Objectives

Drawing upon a personal evaluation, establish objectives for enhancing time management skills.

The attainment of these goals necessitates the adoption of objectives that are well-defined, quantifiable, attainable, pertinent, and time-constrained, commonly referred to as SMART objectives.

Establish achievable objectives that target the primary areas of development identified in the self-evaluation.

For instance, in the event that you have acknowledged that you encounter challenges in prioritizing tasks, the objective could be articulated as follows: "Enhance the aptitude for prioritization by effectively recognizing the most crucial tasks on a daily basis."

Developing Positive Habits

After the establishment of improvement goals, it is imperative to cultivate constructive routines that bolster effective time management.

Please be aware that the process of forming habits requires a considerable amount of time and dedication. However, it is important to recognize that this commitment can result in substantial transformations over an extended period.

Develop an actionable strategy for every improvement goal.

As an illustration, in case your objective entails enhancing self-discipline, it is advisable to meticulously design day-to-day actions that foster discipline, such as setting well-defined deadlines for task completion or implementing incentivization methods to drive the attainment of goals.

Engaging in favorablebehaviors such as obtaining sufficient rest, maintaining a well-balanced nutritional regimen, and engaging in physical activity can substantially enhance your capacity to proficiently regulate and allocate time.

Segmenting Objectives into Achievable Duties

The process of dividing objectives into easily achievable tasks is an essential and integral aspect of efficient time management. It entails the process of systematically decomposing your overarching objectives into smaller, attainable tasks that facilitate your advancement towards the fulfillment of your broader goals. Presented below are several guidelines for dissecting objectives into feasible tasks:

1. Commence by delineating your overarching aspirations: Initiate the process by identifying your broader goals or objectives. These objectives and goals can encompass either long-term

aspirations or short-term ambitions that you aim to accomplish. As an illustration, should your overarching objective revolve around the introduction of a novel product, it would be prudent to decompose it into more manageable intervals.

2. Determine the essential tasks: Determine the essential tasks or activities that are requisite for attaining your overarching objectives. It is imperative that these steps be precise and capable of being acted upon, as they must make a meaningful contribution to the achievement of your overarching objective. As an illustration, assuming that your objective entails the introduction of a novel product, essential undertakings might encompass undertaking market analysis, formulating product design, and strategizing a comprehensive marketing approach.

3. Arrange your tasks in order of priority: Once you have determined the essential tasks, organize them based on

their significance and immediacy. This facilitates concentration on the tasks that are of utmost importance in attaining your objective.

4. Divide tasks into smaller segments: Segment each task into more easily manageable components. This enables them to be effectively handled and mitigates their perceived intimidation. As an illustration, if your assigned objective entails the execution of market research, it would be prudent to partition the task into discrete tasks such as identifying the designated target demographic, formulating a comprehensive survey, and subsequently scrutinizing the obtained data.

5. Establish time limits: Establish specific time limits for every task or sub-task to facilitate your adherence to a structured schedule and verify continuous advancement towards your objective.

6. Monitor progress: Maintain diligent oversight of your advancement towards

accomplishing your objectives and fulfilling your responsibilities. This facilitates your ability to adhere to your objectives and adapt your strategy as needed.

As an illustration, in the event that your overarching objective entails the introduction of a novel product, you can delineate it into constituent tasks such as:

* Undertake market analysis within a two-week timeframe
• Determine the intended demographic (due date: within seven days)
• Construct a questionnaire (time limit: 48 hours)
• Conduct data analysis within a one-week timeframe

Please proceed with the design of the product, ensuring completion within a period of one month.

• Research resources (deadline: two weeks)
• Generate prototypes (due date: within a three-week timeframe)

Develop a comprehensive marketing strategy (target completion: within a fortnight)
- Specify communication channels (deadline: within one week)
- Crafting communication strategies (due date: within a week)

In summary, the process of decomposing objectives into achievable endeavors is a crucial aspect of optimizing time allocation. By commencing with broader objectives, discerning imperative undertakings, prioritizing said undertakings, subdividing them into more manageable components, establishing distinct benchmarks, and vigilantly overseeing advancement, one can steadily advance towards marketing and attain triumph.

Teamwork Is Difficult

Despite the convenience of connecting with team members through multiple platforms, at times, it engenders increased difficulty in collaborating with them. This is because there exists the possibility that not all members of the team may possess a complete commitment or dedication towards the virtual meeting. It is possible that they are encountering external distractions that hinder their level of engagement, or alternatively, they may be experiencing fatigue towards the frequency of online meetings. Certain teams exhibit enhanced performance when they are physically co-located, facilitating dynamic exchange and brainstorming of ideas. This is where hybrid work arrangements prove to be advantageous.
Burnout
The final drawback associated with remote work pertains to the potential

for experiencing burnout. There exists a potential of excessive productivity when carrying out tasks remotely. Insufficient demarcation between work and personal life can result in work encroaching upon one's personal time. Given the current circumstance of working remotely, there is an ample amount of additional time at your disposal. If this surplus of time is not utilized effectively, it is plausible that you may inadvertently prolong your working hours. Engaging in this activity consecutively is ill-advised, as it will eventually result in exhaustion and reduced productivity. Additionally, you would not desire for your residence to become a locale that you grow to detest due to the excessive amount of labor involved. Work never ends. If such is the case, it implies that you are currently out of work. Irrespective of the extent of your efforts today, you will inevitably have a greater workload awaiting you in the forthcoming days. Establishing attainable objectives will help you maintain focus and serve as a timely reminder to take breaks when necessary.

The aforementioned are the drawbacks of remote work. Should you be encountering any of these circumstances, there is no cause for concern. The aforementioned disadvantages can be effectively mitigated through the implementation of the following measures, as outlined. Prior to delving into them, however, I would also like to present the benefits of remote work. This will provide you with a comprehensive understanding of the benefits that working from home can offer.

Benefits of Telecommuting

The greatest benefit of remote work lies in the aspect of time, making effective time management imperative. There are additional significant advantages to remote work resulting from enhanced productivity and increased availability of time.

It Saves Money

Think about it. If it were not necessary for you to commute to the workplace on a daily basis? Transportation expenses, meals, caffeinated beverages, professional attire, and even miscellaneous food items accumulate rapidly. I was unaware of the significant expenditure incurred on my daily commute's coffee. Indeed, a significant portion of the American population remains unaware that abstaining from the daily purchase of coffee presents an opportunity to accumulate savings in the range of $1,000 to $2,000 annually (Rosen, 2020). Given the current surge in food and fuel prices, have you considered the substantial cost savings that could be realized through the adoption of a remote work arrangement? It confers a significant benefit.

You are afforded the opportunity to personalize your surroundings.

Occasionally, while engaged in work, we may require a modicum of inspiration or solace. This could take the shape of cherished quotations, keepsakes, musical selections, or perhaps images capturing the presence of our beloved ones. Nevertheless, it is possible that an office or cubicle environment could be inadequate in accommodating such a preference. It is possible that you may experience unease when your colleagues peruse your belongings. When engaging in remote work, individuals possess the liberty to personalize their work environment according to their preferences and requirements.

No Commuting

Yes. I will reiterate this point due to the substantial advantages it offers. The absence of a daily commute to work confers a significant benefit. You will have the opportunity to enjoy sufficient rest without the need for early wake-up calls and the concerns associated with arriving home late due to traffic congestion. Additionally, your overall disposition will be enhanced. Furthermore, abstaining from commuting to the workplace greatly diminishes both your personal carbon footprint and that of your company. Observe the demonstrable impact of decreased vehicular congestion on the reduction of greenhouse gas emissions and the consequent enhancement of air quality in urban areas worldwide.

Effectively express explicit boundaries to uphold regulations.

Establishing a sense of self-discipline and accountability in your child is contingent upon the existence of a clearly outlined and consistently upheld code of conduct. It is noteworthy that children as young as two years old can remarkably comprehend and comply with uncomplicated instructions.

In order to cultivate a supportive and organized atmosphere, it is imperative to undertake the following measures:

● Clarify the rules of the household: Commence by dedicating time to clearly communicate the established regulations of your residence to your children. This affords them a clear understanding of your expectations and boundaries. Utilize language and examples that are suitable for their age to guarantee their comprehension of the rules and their significance.

● Place importance on uniformity: Uniformity plays a crucial role in establishing rules. It is imperative that every member of the family maintains cohesion and uniformly upholds the same set of rules. This cohesive stance fosters an atmosphere characterized by unambiguous and consistent expectations.

● Modify regulations as time progresses: As your child develops and matures, their obligations and abilities undergo transformation. As a result, it may be necessary to make modifications to your regulations to accommodate these alterations. Participate in transparent and suitable conversations with your child when it appears fitting to adjust current regulations.

Well-defined and consistently applied regulations enable children to cultivate self-discipline. Through gaining an awareness of the ramifications of their actions and adhering to established protocols, they acquire the ability to effectively manage their impulses and conduct.

Regulations establish a structured framework for accountable conduct. They impart upon children the principles of responsibility for their actions and decisions. As they mature, the significance of this sense of responsibility takes on greater importance in their overall development.

Clearly articulated regulations offer well-defined guidance for your child. They possess a clear understanding of the expectations placed upon them, thereby diminishing any potential confusion and alleviating anxiety. This explicitness enhances the coherence of the familial setting.

The establishment of a reliable and predictable adherence to the principles ensures the development of a sense of confidence and reliability in the relationship between the mother figure and the child. When children observe the consistent and equitable application of regulations, they cultivate a sense of confidence in the familial framework and their mother's authority.

Establishing distinct limits is essential when it comes to fostering responsible and self-disciplined offspring. By elucidating these regulations, upholding uniformity, and adjusting them as your progeny progresses in age, you establish an atmosphere that nurtures wholesome growth and proficient discourse.

These rituals not only cultivate indispensable life proficiencies but also foster a sense of cohesion and reliance within the family unit.

Real-World Applications Of The Pomodoro Technique

The Pomodoro technique, forged by Francesco Cirillo during the 1980s, is a method of time management designed to enhance efficacy and the caliber of output. Now, we shall proceed to examine several illustrative instances that exemplify the practical application of this technique in everyday situations.

Example 1: Study

Imagine if you were required to prepare for a crucial examination. You compartmentalize your study materials into segments that can be accomplished within approximately 25-minute intervals. One can establish a timer, commonly referred to as a "pomodoro" (which is the Italian term for "tomato," denoting the kind of kitchen timers employed by Francesco Cirillo), for a duration of 25 minutes in order to commence the process of studying. Throughout this period, it is imperative that you dedicate your undivided attention to your assigned task and refrain from any forms of disturbance. After the timer has elapsed, you may proceed to a brief recess lasting for five minutes. This iteration of the \"pomodoro\" cycle is performed four times, following which a more extended break of approximately 15 to 30 minutes is taken. By the close of the day, you will have not only engaged in more efficient study practices, but you will also have incorporated periodic intervals of rest to mitigate fatigue.

Example 2: Work Projects

Envision yourself as a software developer engaged in the development of an extensive project. There exists a multitude of diverse tasks that necessitate your attention, ranging from the composition of code to the resolution of software defects to the verification of software functionality. By employing the Pomodoro technique, a systematic approach can be adopted whereby tasks are divided into intervals of 25 minutes, thereby enabling one to concentrate on a single task exclusively and subsequently taking brief respites prior to commencing the subsequent task. This facilitates the maintenance of a sustainable work rhythm, thus mitigating the potential sense of being overwhelmed that often accompanies the undertaking of a substantial project.

Example 3: Housework

Engaging in domestic tasks such as maintaining cleanliness and tending to laundry can appear to be a daunting endeavor when perceived in its entirety. Nevertheless, by employing the Pomodoro method, you can divide these tasks into smaller, more achievable fragments. As an alternative, you may consider dedicating a particular time period, commonly known as a "pomodoro," to clean the bathroom prior to taking a brief intermission of five minutes, after which you can proceed with cleaning the kitchen. This methodology has the potential to alleviate the tedium of household chores and effectively thwart procrastination tendencies.

Example 4: Creative Activities

For individuals possessing a skill set in writing, artistic endeavors, or music, the application of the Pomodoro technique can prove invaluable in surmounting periods of stagnation and bolstering overall efficiency. As an illustration, in the context of composing a novel, one may allocate a specific \\\"pomodoro\\\" solely to the development of a character, followed by another dedicated to outlining a scene, and so forth. This approach facilitates undivided attention on individual tasks, which may enhance creative thinking and alleviate feelings of being inundated.

The Pomodoro Technique is versatile in its applicability to a broad range of tasks and projects, proving particularly advantageous in handling extensive or daunting assignments. By partitioning these tasks into smaller time segments, it facilitates your concentration on the present task and enables you to incorporate periodic intervals for rest in order to prevent exhaustion. As demonstrated through these illustrations, the Pomodoro Technique can serve as a valuable asset in enhancing productivity and efficiency across various domains of one's life.

Time Analysis: Mapping the Allocation of Your Time

Engaging in a time audit is a valuable method to acquire perspective regarding one's current allocation of time. It facilitates the identification of unproductive activities and areas amenable to enhancement in one's time management. Presented below is a comprehensive sequential manual outlining the procedure for conducting a time audit:

Firstly, Establish Definitive Goals

Prior to commencing the time audit, it is imperative to clearly establish your objectives. What are your intended outcomes or objectives for carrying out the audit? Are you seeking to enhance efficiency, cultivate a harmonious work-life equilibrium, or identify avenues for skills enhancement? Establishing distinct objectives will serve as a guiding framework for your audit.

Secondly, Select a Timeframe

Please ascertain the desired duration for which the time audit shall be carried out. The duration of the analysis varies depending on the objectives and preferences, ranging from a single day to a whole month. A one-week audit is frequently an advantageous initial step in order to obtain a representative selection of your usual activities.

Proceed to Step 3: Generate a Chronological Record

Utilize a notepad, electronic spreadsheet, or dedicated time-tracking application to generate a comprehensive record of allotted time. Establish columns or compartments to organize the subsequent pieces of information:

● Date: Document the date associated with every entry.

● Commencement time: Please record the exact time at which you initiate each activity.

● Activity: Provide a comprehensive description of the task or activity you are currently involved in.

● Timeframe: Document the duration of each activity. One may employ a stopwatch or timer as a means to enhance precision.

- Classification: Assign activities to distinct categories (e.g., professional, personal, recreational, unproductive).

Step 4: Record Everything

During the designated period you have selected, meticulously document each and every activity you partake in. Please provide comprehensive specifics and endeavor to complete all tasks, regardless of their perceived insignificance. This encompasses professional obligations, personal undertakings, intervals of rest, and even diversions such as examining social media platforms.

Step 5: Practice Transparency and Precision

In order to obtain a precise view of your time management, it is imperative that you candidly assess the manner in which you allocate and utilize your time. Please refrain from modifying your routine solely due to the audit being conducted. The objective is to accurately capture your customary conduct.

Proceed to the sixth step, which involves conducting a thorough analysis of the gathered data.

Once a sufficient amount of data has been accumulated (typically spanning at least a week), it is now appropriate to undertake the examination and interpretation of the findings. Search for consistent patterns, discern trends, and identify areas in which your time is being effectively utilized, as well as those in which it is being unproductively squandered.

● Determine the overall duration allocated to distinct categories (such as work, personal activities, leisure, and unproductive pursuits).

● Determine the specific activities that consume a significant amount of your time or divert your attention.

● Reflect upon whether you are devoting sufficient time to tasks that hold great importance.

Step 7: Engage in introspection and implement necessary modifications

In light of your analysis, ponder upon your findings and contemplate the implementation of modifications to your daily regimen. Are there any responsibilities that you can assign to others or remove entirely? Could you dedicate additional time to significant activities or objectives? Utilize your discernment to enhance your proficiency in managing time.

Proceed to Step 8: Establish Objectives and Track the Advancement

Establish precise objectives for time management, drawing from the insights derived from the audit. Devise a comprehensive strategy to incorporate these modifications seamlessly into your everyday schedule. Consistently assess your progress and make necessary modifications to continually enhance your time management.

Conducting a time audit can be an influential method for enhancing self-awareness and developing efficient time management abilities. It has the potential to facilitate the process of making well-informed decisions regarding the optimal utilization of one's time.

Real-World Applications Of The Pomodoro Technique

This chapter delves into pragmatic strategies that can assist you in effectively managing the difficulties posed by digital overload while maintaining your focus on attaining your objectives. We will explore effective techniques to handle digital diversions, encompassing notifications and allurements from social media platforms, enabling you to regain focus and augment your efficiency. Furthermore, we shall provide assistance in establishing an environment devoid of distractions, conducive to the optimal flourishing of deep work, thus allowing you to fully engage in tasks without any interruptions. Additionally, we will examine the significance of establishing sound boundaries in the modern era of information, enabling you to achieve equilibrium between maintaining connectivity and safeguarding your psychological welfare. Through the implementation of these prescribed strategies, individuals can regain command over their digital sphere and redirect their attention towards matters of true significance.

Strategies for Effectively Handling Digital Interruptions and Distractions

In a society characterized by incessant technological interferences, it is imperative to possess a repertoire of methodologies to effectively tackle digital distractions. By implementing measures such as muting notifications during work hours and employing website blockers for specified intervals, individuals can effectively reclaim their focus and attention. By consciously determining the timing and manner in which you engage with technology, you can diminish the incessant disruptions and establish an environment conducive to concentrated, uninterrupted productivity.

Establishing an Environment Conducive to Uninterrupted Concentration

Envision the possession of a specifically designated area where your concentration flourishes and interferences are effectively mitigated. This constitutes the ideology behind the establishment of a zone free from any kind of distraction. One possibility is: "You may identify a designated space within your residence or a particular section within your professional environment, where you dedicate yourself to undertaking intense, undisturbed endeavors." By consciously establishing such a designated area, you communicate to your mind that it is the appropriate moment to focus, thereby facilitating a remarkable increase in productivity by eliminating the persistent distractions posed by digital elements.

Establishing Effective Boundaries in the Era of Information Technology

As the era of information continues to evolve, establishing boundaries assumes increasing significance. Implementing appropriate restrictions on the amount of time spent on screens, managing email usage, and moderating interactions on social media platforms can effectively mitigate the risk of overwhelming oneself with excessive information and mental exhaustion. Through the establishment of dedicated time slots for digital interaction and the cultivation of intervals devoted to abstaining from technology, one is able to achieve a state of equilibrium whereby they can both remain well-informed and prioritize their personal well-being.

By integrating these methodologies into your everyday schedule, you can revolutionize your interaction with technology and bolster your capacity to concentrate on matters of genuine significance. The goal is not to outright dismiss the digital realm, but rather to conscientiously navigate it, ensuring that technology functions as a facilitator to help achieve your objectives, rather than becoming a perpetual source of diversion. As you undertake the voyage of acquiring expertise in managing digital diversions, you will unveil a newfound sense of lucidity and efficacy in your pursuits. Stay focused and empowered!

Planning And Goal-Setting Effectively: Matching Objectives With Time Allocative

Introduction: Setting goals and engaging in strategic planning go hand in hand with effective time management. This chapter explores the skill of developing a thorough plan and establishing precise objectives that complement the time allotted. Through the development of a methodical planning and goal-setting strategy, readers can enhance their concentration, efficiency, and accomplishments in their personal and professional pursuits.

The Function of Goal-Setting and Planning in Time Management:

Setting goals and making plans give you the foundation for efficient time management. This section discusses the significance of matching goals with available time and looks at how planning can help you use your time more purposefully and with more focus.

Setting Clear Priorities: Those who plan well are able to identify their top priorities and set aside time for them.

Increasing Focus: Establishing goals aids people in maintaining their attention on activities that support their long-term goals.

Encouraging Efficiency: By arranging work in a sensible order, planning helps people make the most of their time.

Minimizing Overwhelm: By dividing large jobs into smaller, more manageable activities, a well-organized strategy helps lessen feelings of overwhelm.

Increasing Decision-Making Capability: Well-defined objectives and a comprehensive strategy help people make better decisions by letting them know which tasks are most important to achieving their goals.

Developing a Comprehensive Plan: The process of developing a comprehensive plan to efficiently manage time is covered in this section. The ability to evaluate long-term objectives, deconstruct them into manageable phases, and create a workable plan of action will be imparted to readers.

Evaluating Extended-Term Goals: defining broad objectives in a range of spheres of life, including relationships, work, personal growth, and health.

Specifying Objectives: establishing SMART goals—specific, measurable, achievable, relevant, and time-bound.

Goal-Breaking: To monitor progress, break down overarching objectives into more manageable, shorter benchmarks.

Setting Priorities: Arranging objectives in order of significance and urgency to allot time appropriately.

Identifying Resources: Evaluating the time, expertise, and assistance needed to accomplish each goal.

Making a Timeline: Putting together a reasonable schedule for completing each stage and ultimate objective.

Aligning Objectives with Time Allocation: This section explores how to align objectives with time allocation after they have been established. To guarantee steady progress, readers will discover how to fit their goals into their daily, weekly, and monthly agendas.

Setting daily goals is incorporating goal-related tasks into everyday activities.

Weekly Progress Review: Setting aside time every week to review the plan, identify obstacles, and gauge progress.

Establishing monthly benchmarks can help you monitor your overall progress toward your long-term objectives.

Setting Up Time Blocks: To guarantee focused attention, set aside certain time slots for completing each goal.

Strategic time management is the key to juggling several priorities without being overburdened.

Creating The Ideal Calendar

The calendar's dates are closer than they seem! What prevents everything from happening at once is time. One day, your diary will keep you.

West Mae

A to-do list is essentially the cream we consume on a daily basis after churning a lot of milk to achieve significant goals and objectives in our lives or at work. Thus, we need to keep a weekly, monthly, or annual calendar in order to provide a foundation or identity for those major aims and objectives. A calendar forces us to think long-term, whereas a to-do list addresses the real, practical issues we confront and how to address them in the immediate term. In addition, it aids in the planning, execution, evaluation, and modification of strategies in light of immediate outcomes or performances. We are just responding in the short term in the absence of a calendar. It provides us with a proactive outlook on life. It is forward planning. Put more succinctly, making sure we don't neglect to complete significant duties in the future—at least not with the things we can control.

In this case, it fulfills a crucial function by preventing duplication when two or more appointments or tasks are combined. If a task conflicts with another task, at least you know what to do about it. When it comes to breaking down goals into actions, a calendar can be used as a form of lighthouse. Kindly refrain from writing your objectives or aspirations on this calendar. Put the time limit and the goals, objectives, etc. on a different sheet. However, something should only be added to a calendar after it has been transformed into a concrete, workable task.

For instance:

Write a report on how staff members are improving their learning capacities. must be turned in two months from now.

It's a goal, and goals shouldn't be put in writing on a calendar and then forgotten after two months. Instead, it could look like this in the calendar:

September 1st: begin the report

Write the second chapter starting on September 8 and continue until November 1st to finish the report and send it.

A calendar is only a to-do list expanded to include weeks, months, and years. After a year, chores become difficult to put into a calendar. Write down everything that comes to mind or that you wish to accomplish on the calendar. It could also happen that the chores lose their significance or relevance by the time you get to that day, which could be three months later.

We could have specific long-term goals in our careers. For example, finish a project or course, pick up a new skill, or organize your year's worth of work. You are able to write each one. There may be times when you feel like you have a lot of information to record in a calendar, but the days seem far ahead of you. Only the most recent tasks have been completed. That is quite typical.

How To Beat Procrastination

Finding the Reasons Behind Procrastination

One typical issue with time management is procrastination. Finding the source of the problem is essential to solving it. Procrastination can be brought on by a variety of emotions and feelings, including overwhelm, perfectionism, fear of failing, and a lack of enthusiasm. By comprehending the reasons behind your procrastination, you may devise tactics to tackle these fundamental problems.

Techniques for Overcoming Procrastination

You can overcome procrastination by using the following useful strategies:

✓ Establish definite dates and objectives: A sense of urgency is created when projects have definite deadlines.

✏ Divide work into manageable chunks: To make bigger activities less daunting, break them down into smaller, more doable ones.

✓ Apply constructive criticism: Give yourself a reward when you finish a task on schedule.

Minimize interruptions: Reduce distractions and establish a concentrated workspace.

We've spoken about these techniques in this chapter to help you beat procrastination and complete your assignment on time.

Chapter 7: Handling Diversion

Typical Workplace Diversions

Distractions have a big effect on how well you manage your time. Frequent sources of workplace distractions include social media use, incessant email notifications, loud work settings, and lengthy meetings. Effectively managing these distractions begins with acknowledging them.

Techniques for Reducing Distractions

Take into account the following tactics to reduce distractions:

Set work priorities: Prioritize critical chores before lower priority ones.

✏ Designate certain times for work: Set aside dedicated periods of time for work. Employ tools for productivity: During working hours, block websites or apps that are distracting.

✓ Express boundaries: Inform your coworkers when you require unbroken work time.

You may improve your focus and productivity by putting these methods into practice and setting up a distraction-free workstation.

The subsequent chapters will cover time management tools and applications, stress management and work-life balance strategies, and effective communication and collaboration techniques.

Techniques for Monitoring Objectives and Responsibility

Progress can be monitored in a variety of ways. In fact, a former coworker used to write a slogan on a Post-it note after finishing a task at work. A couple others have agendas and to-do lists, and one even employed an extremely intricate flowchart that looked like a mental map.

To-do lists are straightforward but efficient. They might even be a little too corny! On the other hand, a to-do list and the Eisenhower Matrix together can be quite effective. This is particularly true if we include an appropriate system of rewards in the mix. A visual queue, for example, is a powerful incentive. An approach utilizing paperclips is one that James Clear discussed in his 2018 book Atomic Habits. In closing, he said, "Making progress is rewarding, and tangible indicators of your progress, such as moving marbles, paperclips, or hairpins, are easy to see. They thereby encourage your conduct and give each activity a tiny boost of instant gratification. You are welcome to try this or other to-do applications that have an eye-catching design.

We gain by tracking our success, even in small ways. It teaches us about ourselves. It is simpler, for instance, to say "no" when a task doesn't fit with our objectives. We may even learn from it and become more adept at adjusting to our daily lives. But it's crucial to use caution. In a globalized culture, unforeseen issues are the norm rather than the exception. This makes the flexibility we discussed while defining our objectives even more crucial. This means that a work we used to consider significant has become a priority, and we need to review our schedule and optimize where everything fits in. Tasks can also become urgent out of the blue. As your time management skills improve, avoid the tendency to become inflexible.

Try to assess your goals on a frequent basis to ensure that you stay adaptable. This is not something that happens every day. For instance, I enjoy returning every two weeks to make adjustments. By then, I usually have advanced enough to see what I'm missing. But you don't have to take that example to heart. It is feasible to check once a week, once a month, or even once every two months. as long as you remain impartial and consistent throughout. Adapting your goals to match reality is typically a more fruitful strategy than trying to ignore it till it fits your agenda once more. Although it can highlight areas of discomfort, time management is ultimately a useful tool.

If you are not flawless at this, that's okay too. A study by Pammer V. et al. suggests that just keeping track of your time will be beneficial. When students started keeping track of their time, both those with and without specialized coaching shown a discernible increase in time management behaviors. Their brief yet fascinating paper had a few more intriguing discoveries. Research showed that there were no extra technical advantages to having a coach help students learn time management skills. On the other hand, these specialists raised the rate of skill retention. Notably, complex concepts were not the source of this discrepancy. Active goal setting, which you've heard about in this chapter, was encouraged for the coached group, and it made a huge difference.

Thus, the best course of action is to combine tracking with specific targets. That aligns very well with the SMART goal criteria, as you may recall. Measurability depends on benchmarks. Our perception plays a significant role in determining how we measure time, which is another topic we'll cover in the upcoming Chapter. You ought to come away from this chapter with a greater comprehension of how individuals take in and interpret environmental cues. In addition, you'll discover methods for customizing the perspective you have on the world. There are various benefits to this.

Practically speaking, none of the methods should be very challenging. At

first, they could be uncomfortable. They could also be challenging to perform regularly. But with experience, they'll come naturally to you. The best thing about it all is how easy these tactics are to use once you know how to do them. Although it takes time to become more aware and thoughtful, you can start by investing some time.
ment as small as 15 minutes daily. So, let's keep going, shall we?

Effective Schedule Design And Planning

Strategic plan: Strategically allocate your time on a weekly and monthly basis to devote to your household tasks and objectives.

In today's interconnected world characterized by numerous distractions and conflicting obligations, the mastery of proficient planning and scheduling has become imperative. This informational publication, entitled "Efficient Planning and Scheduling," will serve as your guide when pursuing professional advancement, organizing a busy household, or striving to accomplish personal goals. We will guide you on a journey to develop a weekly and monthly itinerary that not only allocates time for your obligations and objectives but also empowers you to regain authority over your life.

Strategizing and Organizing: A Fine Craft

Acknowledge the criticality of meticulous planning and meticulous scheduling in achieving success.

Uncover the tangible benefits of achieving success in time management.

Putting the Groundwork in

Acquire knowledge about the techniques and resources that could aid you in your endeavors of planning and scheduling.

To facilitate effective time management, establish and determine your individual objectives and aspirations.

A Recommended Weekly Schedule for Your Consideration

Examine the sequential process for generating a weekly timetable.

To ensure optimal efficacy, it is advisable to explore various methodologies and approaches for time management through the implementation of time-blocking techniques.

The Mastery of Monthly Planning

Acknowledge the importance of adopting a broad, inclusive perspective.

Discover proper methods for aligning your weekly agenda with your overarching monthly objectives.

Your Life in Balance

Uncover the significance of the expression "work-life balance" and its correlation with your schedule.

Acquire strategies for maintaining high levels of motivation during the pursuit of your objectives.

Task Management That Works

Discover methods for turning your aspirations into doable chores.

To optimize your time utilization, employ efficient task prioritization techniques.

Strategies for Effective Management of Unforeseen Changes

Prepare yourself for unexpected events and disruptions, as they are bound to occur.

Develop strategies to modify your timetable while upholding your goals.

Supervising Your Advancement and Modifying Your Course

Acquire the skills to assess your progress and identify opportunities for improvement.

As you gain knowledge, contemplate methods to enhance your schedule.

Time management in psychology

Acquire further insights into the cognitive aspects of effective time allocation.

Inclination towards delaying tasks and persistent cognitive impediments to surmount.

Authentic Accounts of Achievement

Observe and learn from those who have enhanced their lives through careful planning and adherence to a structured regimen.

Discover the strategies they employ to surmount challenges in order to achieve their aspirations.

Formulating a strategic plan and establishing a structured routine for one's lifestyle.

Acquire the skills necessary to incorporate planning and scheduling into your daily regimen.

Discover techniques for optimizing time management through advanced methodologies.

Effective Time Management Strategies for Entrepreneurs

Optimal strategies for prioritizing tasks and efficiently managing time

In light of your position as a business proprietor, you are burdened with a multitude of tasks, posing the formidable challenge of efficiently balancing your manifold responsibilities. Effective time management strategies can assist individuals in prioritizing tasks and optimizing their time utilization, resulting in the attainment of objectives and heightened levels of productivity. In the following chapter, we will explore several optimal approaches to prioritizing tasks and effectively managing time.

1. Create a To-Do List

A highly efficient and straightforward approach to managing one's time is the creation of a comprehensive agenda or task schedule. Begin each day by compiling a roster of the duties that require your attention, subsequently arranging them in order of significance and immediacy. This approach will aid in maintaining your concentration and guaranteeing that you prioritize your utmost essential tasks.

2. Use the 80/20 Rule

The principle commonly referred to as the 80/20 rule, alternatively known as the Pareto principle, asserts that approximately 80% of the outcomes you attain stem from roughly 20% of the inputs or actions you exert. Implement this principle within your professional endeavors by discerning the tasks that contribute significantly to the success of your business entity, and channeling your time and effort towards these specific tasks.

3. Prioritize Difficult Tasks First

It is quite common to become ensnared in the habit of postponing challenging assignments, yet such behavior can result in heightened levels of stress and diminished levels of productivity. Instead, give precedence to your most formidable tasks during the early hours of the day, when your energy and concentration levels are at their optimum.

4. Set Realistic Goals

Establishing unattainable objectives could result in feelings of disillusionment and exhaustion. Rather, establish realistic objectives that present both a stimulating and feasible level of difficulty. Divide overarching objectives into more easily achievable subtasks, and acknowledge and appreciate your advancements as you proceed.

5. Eliminate Time-Wasters

Disturbances like social media, electronic mail, and phone calls can consume a considerable portion of your daily schedule. Discern the tasks which hold the highest potential for diverting your attention, and implement measures to eliminate or curtail their impact.

6. Use Time-Blocking

Time-blocking entails allocating dedicated time intervals for each task listed on your agenda. This methodology can assist in maintaining focus and ensuring adequate time allocation for each individual task.

7. Delegate Tasks

Allocation of tasks is a pivotal element in effective time management. Identify and assign tasks that can be accomplished by members of your team, thereby allowing you to allocate your time to more pressing responsibilities.

Optimizing the Efficient Utilization of Your Time

T

Time is a valuable asset that, once lost, cannot be reclaimed. In order to attain success and achieve our objectives, it is of utmost importance to acquire the skill of effectively managing our time.

Determining Priorities:

One of the key elements in effective time management pertains to identifying which tasks deserve priority. This necessitates the identification of priority tasks and their prompt resolution before attending to any other matters.

There exist approaches to the prioritization of tasks. One method involves the utilization of the Eisenhower Matrix, which entails the categorization of tasks into four distinct classifications; "

● Immediate attention required: These tasks necessitate prompt action.

● Non-urgent: These tasks are able to be deferred, however, they still retain a level of importance.

● Inconsequential: These tasks possess minimal importance, yet still require attention.

● Trivial and non-urgent: These tasks can be overlooked or dismissed.

An alternative approach for prioritization is the utilization of the ABCDE technique. This particular method involves the classification of tasks into five distinct groups;

● Group A: These tasks carry significant importance and require immediate attention.

● Group B: These tasks hold significant importance. Less time-critical compared to those in Group A.

● Group C: These tasks hold significant significance. Still requires attention.

● Group D: These tasks can be assigned to an individual for execution.

● Group E: These tasks are open to elimination.

The Mastery of Refusal: "

An additional vital component of proficient time management entails acquiring the mastery of the art of declining requests or invitations. It necessitates the ability to politely refuse requests for your time that are not in accordance with your priorities.

Declining can pose difficulties, particularly when one possesses a willingness to assist. Nevertheless, it is crucial to bear in mind that one cannot assume the responsibility for everything. Consistently agreeing to every request will eventually result in experiencing a sense of being overwhelmed and burdened by stress.

Minimizing Distractions:

Managing time can be impeded by various forms of distractions. They consume your time. Divert your focus.

To mitigate distractions, please take into account these strategies;

● Ensure that your phone and computer are powered off while engaged in a task.

● Locate a setting conducive to minimal disruptions. ● Identify a place where the likelihood of interruptions is low. ● Seek out a venue that is unlikely to be disrupted.

● Designate specific time slots for the purpose of reviewing emails and engaging in social media.

Develop the skill of focusing on a single task exclusively.

Effective Task Delegation:

When confronted with a substantial workload, do not hesitate to assign tasks to fellow colleagues in order to distribute the workload evenly. By implementing this practice, you will be able to optimize time management and focus on essential tasks of utmost importance.

It is of paramount importance to impart clear instructions pertaining to the objectives and deadlines when delegating tasks. Furthermore, it is of equal importance to bestow upon the individual in charge of the assigned duty the requisite power to make decisions.

Efficient Strategies for Alleviating Stress

The proper management of stress entails the careful consideration and nurturing of both your enduring mental and physical well-being. Nevertheless, there are instances where there is limited opportunity to indulge in activities such as taking a nap, embarking on a challenging hike, or immersing oneself in a captivating novel. Therefore, presented below are 25 strategies to alleviate stress within a time frame of five minutes or less. Whether it beindulging in a piece of chocolate or engaging in the practice of meditation, individuals can find a wide array of expedient stress-alleviating strategies.

1. Breathe

Taking slow, deep breaths has the potential to reduce both blood pressure and heart rate. Consider practicing pranayama breathing, which is a yogic technique entailing the rhythmic inhalation and exhalation through alternating nostrils. This method has been known to alleviate symptoms of anxiety. The approach is purported to operate in a similar manner as acupuncture, promoting equilibrium between the mental and physical aspects.

2. Listen to Music

Irrespective of the musical composition, there are instances where passionately vocalizing the lyrics to a cherished melody can create an illusion of contentment. In a public setting, merely engaging in the act of listening to music can serve as an expedient remedy for a negative emotional state. Classical music has the propensity to impart a heightened sense of relaxation, particularly when listened to immediately prior to retiring for the night.

3. Take a Quick Walk

When you find yourself experiencing feelings of being overwhelmed or encountering difficulties in maintaining focus, it is advisable to undertake a brief walk around the vicinity. You will reap the advantages of solitude, engaging in physical exercise, and taking a few moments to collect your thoughts.

4. Find the Sun

If the weather is clear, venture outdoors as a simple means to uplift your mood. Intense illumination can serve as a viable therapeutic intervention for individuals afflicted with depression and may even elicit uplifted moods in individuals otherwise unaffected by the condition.

5. Administer a Self-Initiated Hand Massage

In the absence of a professional masseuse, one may opt to perform a self-administered hand massage to achieve immediate relaxation and alleviate a racing or thumping heartbeat. In general, there is a propensity for hands to accumulate significant levels of tension. Administer a layer of lotion and commence the manipulation of the muscle foundation below the thumb in order to alleviate tension in the areas of the shoulders, neck, and scalp.

6. Count Backward

In instances when concerns are greatly prevalent, attempt the technique of meticulously enumerating from one to ten and subsequently reversing the process in order to restore tranquility. It is more challenging to experience excessive anxiety regarding an impending examination or job interview if you are preoccupied with recalling the numerical value that precedes seven.

7. Stretch

Assuming a more formal tone, one could rephrase the sentence as follows: "Engaging in brief periods of standing and stretching can alleviate muscular tension and facilitate relaxation amidst a demanding work environment." Attempt a maneuver known as the shoulder roll-out or engage in a chest-opening stretch directly from your seated position at the desk.

8. Glide the soles of your feet across a golf ball

A spontaneous and soothing foot massage can be attained by gently gliding your feet back and forth across the surface of a golf ball.

9. Close Your Eyes

Temporarily alleviate the demands of a bustling workplace or a tumultuous domestic environment by simply engaging in the act of gently closing one's eyes. It provides a convenient method for reestablishingtranquility and enhancing concentration.

10. Squeeze a Stress Ball

During occasions where you experience frustration or irritation towards a colleague, flatmate, or a fellow driver, consider utilizing a stress ball as a means to manage and alleviate such emotions. It represents a convenient, portable, and non-aggressive method to alleviate stress.

11. Try Progressive Relaxation

Anxious? Apply pressure, then release, and engage in sequential repetition. To attain a state of tranquility, one employs the technique of progressive relaxation, which entails sequentially contracting the muscles in individual body parts. The technique, which is also employed by actors, is an excellent means to facilitate sleep.

12. Be Alone

A brief period of solitude lasting five minutes can facilitate the gathering of your thoughts and the clearing of your mind.

13. Get Organized

The presence of excess belongings may be augmenting your experience of stress. Please dedicate a few minutes to rearranging your desk (or table, or wherever you are situated), ensuring that only essential items remain on the surface.

14. Do Some Yoga

Rest your feet against the wall, naturally. The ViparitiKirani yoga asana entails reclining on the ground while positioning the legs in an elevated manner against a vertical surface. In addition to providing the body with a beneficial stretching experience, it also contributes to the attainment of mental tranquility.

15. Eat Some Chocolate

Merely a small, approximately 1.4-ounce portion of this confectionery can effectively alleviate one's anxiety. Dark chocolate effectively modulates cortisol levels, thereby promoting metabolic stability.

16. Meditate

A mere five minutes of solitude is sufficient to attain the rewards of practicing meditation. There is empirical evidence to suggest that engaging in two brief sessions of silent meditation on a daily basis has the potential to alleviate stress and depressive symptoms. Locate a tranquil location conducive to relaxation, assume a comfortable position, direct your attention towards your breathing, and perceive the gradual alleviation of those feelings of anxiety.

Setting Goals And Organizing

This chapter will cover the significance of planning and setting priorities in order to maximize output and make the most of our time. Time is money, so if we don't prioritize our responsibilities and make time for them in our schedules, we run the risk of squandering it on unimportant chores or letting crucial ones get overlooked.

Creating a to-do list is the first stage in planning and prioritizing. From the most crucial to the least crucial, this list should contain every task we have to finish. Next, by placing the most crucial tasks at the top and the least crucial tasks at the bottom of the list, we can prioritize it. This makes sure we don't waste time on low-priority tasks and instead focus on the most important ones first.

Time-blocking is an essential component of planning and prioritization. This entails devoting particular time blocks to particular jobs or pursuits. For instance, we could set aside a certain amount of time every day for checking and replying to emails, and another set aside for finishing urgent tasks. We can make sure we don't get sidetracked from our work by setting time blocks.

It's also critical to recognize our patterns and inclinations in order to plan and prioritize tasks efficiently. While some people are most productive in the afternoons or evenings, others are most productive in the mornings. We can avoid wasting time during less productive times by scheduling our most important tasks during our most productive hours by understanding our natural rhythms.

Barack Obama, the former president, is a well-known example of planning and setting priorities. He had a reputation for keeping a strict schedule and exercising extreme self-control with his time. Every day, he would get up early to work out before reading and getting ready for meetings for the first few hours of the day. Putting his health and intellectual development first in the morning allowed him to be more focused and productive the rest of the day.

Setting priorities and making a plan are vital, but so is being adaptive and flexible. Our plans can be derailed by unforeseen circumstances and emergencies, so we must be able to modify our schedules appropriately. We can deal with unforeseen events without compromising our productivity if we allow for some flexibility and leave buffer time between tasks.

To sum up, planning and setting priorities are essential for reaching our objectives and increasing productivity. We can manage our time and make the most of every minute by creating a to-do list, setting priorities, time-blocking, being aware of our rhythms, and maintaining flexibility. Time is money, so we can invest in our futures and lead more satisfying lives by setting priorities and making plans.

Myth 10: Workers Won't Develop Close Personal Bonds

Although it's possible, personal relationships may suffer from remote work. Since it enables them to keep appropriate boundaries between their personal and professional lives while concentrating more intently on their work, many people prefer working remotely. Employees frequently talk about things unrelated to work in the office, sometimes getting sidetracked.

Nonetheless, when working remotely, staff members can still speak with one another via online tools and, if needed, by phone or video chat services like Zoom or Skype. As a result, interpersonal bonds can still develop and grow between remote employees.

Myth 11: More Gatherings Are Required

Meetings conducted virtually are typically more productive and focused than those held in person. Discussions in in-person meetings frequently stray from the subject at hand, which makes them last longer. Employee focus and attention are enhanced by virtual meetings, which are typically shorter and more focused.

When you realize that these issues with remote work are not as big of a deal as you first imagined, you can take the risk of implementing remote work policies and look for ways to make it work for you and your staff. Additionally, you can create systems to allay any remaining worries regarding working remotely.

Task: Enumerate your worries regarding working remotely and consider the underlying causes. Determine how to allay these worries and proceed with assurance in a remote work setting.

Dispelling the misconceptions about working remotely is just the start. In order to fully benefit from remote work, you and your team need to be willing to adapt to these new working conditions. By addressing issues and implementing practical solutions, you can establish a remote work environment that is both productive and fulfilling.

Some Examples And Case Studies Of How These Principles And Strategies Have Worked For Successful People Or Organisations

These principles and strategies have proven effective for a multitude of accomplished individuals and organizations across various fields and industries. Presented below are several illustrations and case studies illustrating the application of these principles and strategies, which have resulted in enhanced time management and productivity levels for their organization.

● Elon Musk: Renowned as the founder and Chief Executive Officer of Tesla and SpaceX, he is widely recognized for his audacious and far-sighted aspirations. He employs the SMART goal-setting methodology to deconstruct his major objectives into smaller, more feasible tasks. An illustration of this would be his determination to achieve the ambitious objective of establishing a human colony on Mars within the timeframe of 2024. To attain this goal, he has strategically divided the mission into various smaller milestones, including the successful launch of the Starship rocket by 2020, the execution of the inaugural crewed mission by 2022, and the establishment of a lasting base by 2024. Additionally, he employs the principle of prioritization to concentrate his attention on the tasks that are of utmost importance and urgency across his various undertakings.

He adheres to a daily itinerary that allots time for engineering, design, meetings, correspondence, and communications, in accordance with their respective levels of importance. In addition, he employs the principle of batching to consolidate similar tasks and execute them concurrently. As an illustration, he allocates Mondays and Fridays to SpaceX, designates Tuesdays and Thursdays for Tesla, and reserves

Wednesdays for his other endeavors. In addition, he employs the elimination principle as a means of eliminating any factors that may detract from his work environment. He is employed in a tranquil and unadorned workplace devoid of windows, embellishments, and telecommunication devices. Additionally, he restricts his usage of social media and refrains from attending unnecessary meetings.

● Oprah Winfrey: Renowned for her remarkable contributions to the media industry as well as her profound impact on societal welfare, this distinguished individual holds a reputation for her exceptional productivity and influential sway. She employs the proactive approach of pre-emptively preparing for her various tasks and objectives. She adheres to a morning regimen which encompasses meditation, physical activity, literary engagement, and expressive reflection in her gratitude log. Additionally, she utilizes a planner to effectively arrange and manage her daily commitments and responsibilities. Additionally, she employs the delegation principle in order to distribute certain tasks to her team members or partners.

She relies upon a dependable team to assist her with various aspects of her media production, business administration, philanthropic endeavors, among other pursuits. Additionally, she employs the principle of automation in order to enhance the efficiency and optimization of various processes and systems in her operations. She employs technology and software for the purpose of overseeing her finances, communications, marketing, and other related domains. Additionally, she employs the principle of elimination to eradicate any diversions from both her personal and professional spheres. She refrains from viewing television, perusing discouraging news reports, or participating in idle rumors. Additionally, she establishes clear limits for her interactions with others and is assertive in declining requests or invitations that do not align with her objectives or principles.

● Amazon: Renowned for its ingenuity and operational excellence, the prominent e-commerce powerhouse continues to be at the forefront of technological advancements. It employs the SMART framework to establish unambiguous and attainable objectives for its offerings. It employs the OKR (Objectives and Key Results) methodology to align its objectives with its overarching vision and mission. Furthermore, this approach employs the prioritization principle to concentrate on the tasks that are of utmost importance and urgency for both its customers and stakeholders. It employs the principle of customer obsession to prioritize the customer's needs in all of its endeavors. Additionally, it adheres to the principle of employing the two-pizza rule, ensuring that its teams consist of no more than 10 individuals. This strategic approach effectively mitigates the expenses incurred by facilitating communication and coordination among team members. It additionally employs the principle of proactive planning, enabling it to foresee forthcoming trends and opportunities. It employs the application of the 10x rule in order to strive for achievements that are ten times superior to those of its competitors. Additionally, it employs the technique of conveying intricate concepts in a straightforward and succinct manner through the utilization of six-page memos. Furthermore, it employs the principle of delegation to bestow authority upon its employees and partners, allowing them to make informed decisions and initiate actions.

It employs the principle of ownership to foster accountability among its employees for their results and outcomes. Furthermore, it employs the principle of batching to consolidate similar tasks and carry them out collectively. It leverages the functionality of the one-click ordering feature to streamline the online shopping experience for its clientele. It additionally employs the principle of automation to streamline certain processes and systems within its operations. It leverages sophisticated technologies such as artificial intelligence, machine learning, robotics, cloud computing, among others, to augment and optimize its operational capabilities, delivery mechanisms, customer service offerings, and more. Additionally, it employs the elimination principle to eradicate waste and inefficiency within its value chain. It applies the lean management principle to eradicate any task or activity that fails to provide value to its customers or stakeholders.

In conclusion, these are a few of the validated principles and strategies for enhancing your time management and productivity capabilities:
- Setting SMART goals
- Prioritising tasks
- Planning ahead
- Delegating and outsourcing

- Batching and automating
- Eliminating distractions

One can make use of these principles and strategies across various domains of life, including but not limited to professional endeavors, educational pursuits, personal residences, physical well-being, recreational interests, and more. This can be achieved by customizing them according to individual requirements, personal inclinations, or situational contexts.

Additionally, one can acquire knowledge from various instances and practical analyses of how these principles and strategies have proven effective for accomplished individuals or reputable entities across diverse sectors and domains.

In the subsequent chapter, we shall present a range of pragmatic suggestions and techniques for incorporating these principles and strategies effectively within your daily regimen. Stay tuned!

Chapter 5: Maintaining Equilibrium and Mitigating Exhaustion

The concept and strategies for accomplishing an optimal work-life equilibrium

Achieving a state of equilibrium between professional and personal obligations is a vital factor in upholding effective time management and evading physical and mental exhaustion. However, what precisely does this equilibrium signify, and how may we attain it?

The concept of work-life balance entails attaining a state of equilibrium wherein an individual effectively allocates their time and energy between occupational responsibilities and personal obligations. It is not merely a question of tallying the hours devoted to each pursuit, but rather of attaining a sense of complete fulfillment in both domains, without allowing one to compromise the other. Put simply, it entails striking the appropriate balance between one's professional endeavors and personal life, enabling them to coexist harmoniously.

The achievement of work-life balance represents a constantly evolving objective, characterized by its adaptable nature, subjective discrepancies between individuals, and potential to undergo transformations throughout one's life. Several elements such as personal circumstances, professional stage, individual demeanor, and personal values can influence an individual's interpretation of work-life balance.

Attaining an optimal equilibrium between professional commitments and personal pursuits can appear formidable, particularly within a progressively interconnected society where the distinction between work and private life has become indistinct. Nevertheless, there are methodologies and principles that can facilitate its attainment.

The initial stage necessitates an introspective evaluation. Every individual must establish their own set of priorities and grasp their true values. What holds the utmost significance in your life? Are you referring to aspects such as your professional trajectory, familial relationships, physical well-being, individual growth, and social interactions? A clear understanding and comprehension in these domains can assist in identifying the appropriate areas where one should allocate their valuable time and energy.

The subsequent course of action entails establishing unambiguous demarcations between professional and personal spheres. This could entail establishing designated working hours and ensuring a clear demarcation between work and leisure time, both physically and mentally. In the era of digitalization, it is particularly advantageous to institute regulations pertaining to the utilization of electronic devices for professional purposes beyond the designated working hours.

Versatility is also an essential element in achieving equilibrium between work and personal life. It is crucial to acknowledge that each week or day may not transpire uniformly and that unforeseen circumstances may arise. Engaging in careful strategic planning can offer advantages, however, it is equally crucial to possess the ability to embrace and accommodate unexpected changes while upholding an open-minded and adaptable perspective.

It is imperative to maintain effective communication not only with superiors but also with colleagues and family members. Effectively conveying your requirements and boundaries to others can facilitate the establishment of reasonable projections and cultivate a nurturing atmosphere.

Self-preservation is an equally crucial component of maintaining a healthy equilibrium between one's professional and personal life. This encompasses aspects of bodily maintenance, like adhering to a nutritious diet and engaging in consistent physical activity, as well as maintaining psychological well-being through practices such as meditation and activities that induce relaxation. Devoting time to self-care can yield advantageous outcomes in both professional and personal spheres.

Finally, delegation can serve as an invaluable mechanism for preserving equilibrium. Rather than attempting to handle all responsibilities independently, it can prove advantageous to assign tasks, be it within one's personal or professional domain. This can enable you to devote your time and attention to the facets of life that hold the highest significance for you.

Achieving a harmonious equilibrium between one's professional and personal spheres may appear daunting, yet it stands as a crucial element of efficient time allocation. By employing a blend of introspection, establishing boundaries, adaptability, effective communication, prioritizing self-care, and sharing responsibilities, it is conceivable to attain a state of equilibrium that facilitates professional accomplishment alongside a gratifying and enriching personal existence.

Attaining Equilibrium Between Professional And Personal Life And Effectively Coping With Stress

The concept of "work-life balance" pertains to achieving equilibrium between one's personal and professional responsibilities, guaranteeing that both areas receive adequate attention and fulfillment. It involves establishing priorities and allocating time and resources to various aspects of one's life, including career, interpersonal connections, family, personal interests, and self-preservation. For the overall welfare, efficiency, and sustained satisfaction, the establishment of a harmonious equilibrium between work and personal life is imperative.

Establishing boundaries and effectively managing one's time are essential in attaining a harmonious equilibrium between professional obligations and personal commitments. Establish clear and definitive working hours and endeavor to strictly abide by them; this will assist in preventing the occurrence of extensive overtime or the transfer of work-related stress into your personal life. Allocate time for your personal pursuits, leisure activities, and self-preservation. Implement effective time management techniques to enhance productivity during working hours and minimize the encroachment of work on personal time. These techniques include prioritizing tasks, delegating responsibilities whenever feasible, and refraining from engaging in multitasking. Strategies for self-care and stress reduction Self-care is vital for effectively managing stress and maintaining a harmonious work-life equilibrium. Place significance on elements such as physical activity, a nutritious dietary regimen, and sufficient rest that effectively contribute to one's overall physical and cognitive welfare. Engage in pleasurable and soothing pursuits, such as personal hobbies, quality time with beloved individuals, or the cultivation of individual interests. In order to minimize feelings of stress and uphold one's emotional well-being, it is advisable to employ stress management techniques such as engaging in deep breathing exercises, practicing meditation, or cultivating mindfulness. One can effectively manage stress and enhance personal well-being.

Promoting overall wellness through the practice of self-care.

Fostering support networks and seeking assistance as needed are essential for the effective management of stress and the maintenance of a healthy work-life equilibrium. Cultivate relationships with colleagues, acquaintances, and relatives who possess the capacity to comprehend, bolster, and motivate you. Communicate your requirements and limitations to those in close proximity so that they may provide the necessary assistance and support. Do not hesitate to seek assistance whenever the situation demands it, whether it entails assigning tasks, seeking professional guidance, or seeking support from trusted friends and family members. One can reduce their workload and decrease their levels of stress by utilizing support systems and seeking aid from others.

Mindfulness and present moment awareness are techniques employed to cultivate a focused state of mind. Embracing the present moment without passing judgment or clinging onto thoughts of the past or future constitutes the essence of mindfulness.

entails. Incorporate mindfulness practices into your everyday routine to cultivate a state of equilibrium and tranquility. For the purpose of remaining present and alleviating stress, one may consider engaging in the practices of diligent eating, attentive strolling, or contemplative meditation. Devote your full focus to your hobbies in order to fully immerse yourself in them and derive maximum enjoyment. By actively participating in mindfulness practices and cultivating a sense of presence, individuals have the potential to enhance their ability to concentrate, reduce their stress levels, and achieve a more harmonious equilibrium between work and personal life.

Effective stress management and achieving work-life balance are continuous endeavors that require conscientious exertion and self-reflection. You are capable of effectively managing your time, establishing personal boundaries, attending to your well-being, regulating stress levels, establishing supportive networks, and participating in mindfulness exercises.

In the subsequent chapters, we shall examine approaches aimed at fostering resilience while making necessary adaptations.

1.3 Methods for Crafting an Efficient Task Agenda

Efficient time management and effective prioritization can be facilitated through the utilization of a meticulously structured task schedule. It facilitates the organization of tasks, establishment of priorities, and retention of concentration. Presented below are several procedural guidelines for the development of a highly efficient task inventory:

1. Comprehensively document all duties: Commence by recording all the tasks that necessitate your attention. This may encompass tasks of a personal nature, professional obligations, and objectives for the future. Ensure that every detail is documented, irrespective of its size or apparent insignificance.

2. Organize tasks into distinct categories, including work-related, personal, family-related, and health-related tasks. This facilitates the attainment of a comprehensive overview concerning the various domains of your life, thereby simplifying the endeavor of managing your responsibilities.

3. Utilize the Eisenhower Matrix: Employ the Eisenhower Matrix to establish

prioritization of your tasks. Allocate each task to one of the four quadrants in accordance with its degree of urgency and significance, as deliberated upon in the preceding subsection.

4. Divide arduous assignments: Divide intricate or time-consuming assignments into smaller, achievable sub-tasks. This facilitates their resolution and enables you to make advancements despite time constraints.

5. Establish target completion dates: Determine specific dates for the completion of each task, even if they are self-imposed. Imposed time constraints engender a heightened sense of urgency, effectively fostering concentration and motivation to fulfill assigned duties.

6. Periodic assessment and revision: Consistently evaluate and revise your task list. Mark off tasks that have been completed and incorporate any additional ones as necessary. This facilitates the maintenance of a precise portrayal of your priorities,

guaranteeing constant awareness of impending tasks.

7. Maintain visibility: Ensure that your to-do list is readily accessible by keeping it prominently displayed, such as on your workstation, mobile device, or utilizing a digital platform like Trello or Todoist. This aids in maintaining concentration and serves as a constant reminder of one's priorities throughout the entirety of the day.

8. Exercise pragmatism: Avoid overwhelming your agenda by incorporating an excessive number of tasks. Maintain a practical outlook regarding your potential accomplishments within a designated period of time. Compiling an excessive number of tasks on your agenda can give rise to sentiments of being inundated and impede your ability to concentrate on essential matters.

C. Strategies for enhancing concentration and enhancing cognitive focus

Enhancing one's level of concentration and focus is crucial in order to attain one's objectives and effectively contribute to productivity. Presented below are a handful of guidelines to enhance your concentration and focus abilities:

Establish distinct objectives: Having a clear understanding of what you aspire to achieve facilitates concentration on the current task and sustains motivation. Establish objectives that are delineated, quantifiable, and realistic for oneself, subsequently subdividing them into more manageable undertakings.

Minimize interruptions: Recognize and minimize any disturbances that hinder your ability to concentrate. This could encompass a range of factors, including alerts on your mobile device and ambient sounds in the surroundings. Please power down your phone or relocate it to a different area, minimize any superfluous browser tabs on your computer, and contemplate employing noise-cancelling headphones should the presence of ambient noise be disruptive.

Observe frequent intervals: Adhering to regular intervals can assist in preventing burnout and maintaining a refreshed state. It is advisable to intermittently engage in brief intervals of rest, occurring approximately every hour, in order to provide respite for both your visual organs and cognitive faculties. Avail yourself of these intervals to engage in stretching exercises, procure a beverage, or engage in any other activity that rejuvenates your mental faculties.

Arrange tasks in order of priority: Organizing your tasks based on their level of importance can aid in maintaining focus on critical objectives. Compile a comprehensive inventory of your assignments and arrange them in order of significance and time sensitivity.

Employ the Pomodoro Technique: This time management methodology, known as the Pomodoro Technique, offers effective means of enhancing productivity and maintaining concentration. The methodology entails decomposing your tasks into shorter, concentrated intervals while incorporating periodic intervals of rest.

Chapter 10: Deadline Management

D
Effective time management is an essential competency that enables one to ensure timely completion of a project. It is imperative to have a comprehensive comprehension of the goals and objectives at hand and establish practical timelines for each respective task.

Efficient deadline control necessitates continual monitoring and assessment of advancements.
This entails consistently evaluating the status of tasks, monitoring progress, and identifying any potential hindrances or impediments.

It is imperative to promptly tackle these issues and implement necessary adaptations to ensure timely completion of tasks.

It is imperative to ensure that these deadlines are effectively communicated to all relevant stakeholders participating in the project.

The implementation of the following suggestions facilitates the efficient management of deadlines:

• Prioritize tasks:
Not all tasks possess equal significance; therefore, it is imperative to give priority to each task based on its level of importance and urgency. Prioritize the most essential tasks and ensure their timely completion.

• Decompose intricate tasks: • Dissect complicated tasks: • Analyze intricate

tasks: • Unravel convoluted tasks: • Dismantle elaborate tasks:
Sizeable undertakings may seem daunting, yet by dissecting them into smaller, more feasible components, they can be rendered less intimidating. Establish specific timelines for each subtask and ensure steady advancement towards the overarching objective.

- Employ resources for efficient deadline management: Various resources can be employed to effectively handle deadlines, including project management software, calendars, and to-do lists. Utilize these instruments to monitor your advancement and remain vigilant regarding time constraints.

• Maintain a high degree of organization: Sustaining a well-structured approach is crucial in effectively managing deadlines. Maintain a pristine and organized workspace, give priority to your tasks, and diligently monitor your deadlines in a centralized manner.

- Communicate with stakeholders: It's important to keep all stakeholders informed of your progress and any issues that may impact the project timeline. Consistently engage in communication with team members and clients to ascertain alignment among all stakeholders.

- Prioritize maintaining work quality alongside meeting deadlines, as both aspects are essential for success. Do not compromise quality by hastily completing tasks. Make careful preparations, maintain order, and allocate sufficient time to generate work of exceptional quality.

By adhering to these guidelines, you can efficiently handle deadlines and successfully attain your objectives without compromising on the overall quality.

In the upcoming section, we will delve into the topic of distractions, exploring strategies for minimizing these disruptions to optimize productivity and timely completion of tasks.

c. The famous work-life balance
The fly is utterly absorbed in its tasks, to the extent that it has overlooked its own identity. Likewise, a subset of individuals parallelly find themselves increasingly preoccupied with professional endeavors, leading to sacrifices in their personal spheres. It is both ironic and unfortunate that we have not achieved success in our professional endeavors nor find contentment in our personal lives. The underlying issue resides in the inadequate management of time.
I began compiling a record of my office expenditures in a Google Spreadsheet. I was astonished to discover that I was expending a significant sum on inconsequential expenditures. Extended

periods of work can contribute to a sense of overconfidence in the availability of time to complete tasks, subsequently leading to a tendency to postpone the completion of critical responsibilities, resulting in a perpetual state of urgency. We will rapidly transition from one emergency to the next. Effective time management can be facilitated through the creation of a schedule or the practice of time boxing, where tasks are allotted specific time slots, or by compiling a comprehensive list of prioritized tasks. Adequate literature and informational materials pertaining to time management are accessible, however the fundamental principles are as follows:

Multi-tasking is a myth. Fostering a state of intense concentration and operating in a state of optimal productivity will contribute to the successful completion of tasks.

Focus on one task at a time and prioritize it as the utmost important. The principle of focusing on one task at a time and completing it diligently is widely acknowledged to be a highly commendable approach.

Adopt the 80/20 rule.

Compose a list of tasks utilizing a digital application or alternatively within a compact personal organizer. This will assist you in ensuring that you do not overlook crucial matters.

Prioritise your tasks. Assign the tasks that require attention to appropriate individuals.

Don't get distracted. Segregate leisure time from professional commitments, in other words, practice compartmentalization.

d. Names are important

Are you acquainted with the auditory sensation that brings the most pleasurable sensation to an individual? I am of the opinion that it is their given name. The name of an individual holds significant importance as it serves as their unique identifier. Consequently, it is imperative to retain and recall the names of individuals. The fly had exerted maximal effort in familiarizing itself with its given appellation. Address individuals using their respective names and, if they hold a higher position or rank, demonstrate courtesy by using appropriate honorifics such as Shri, Sir, Mr, Madam, ji, among others.

If one experiences difficulty recalling names of individuals (similar to myself), there is no issue in politely requesting their names once more. Numerous individuals encounter this issue. Direct your attention to the speaker's name when they are providing you with information. Attempt to visualize their name and establish a mental connection between it and their physical features or visual presentation. Reiterate the name twice or thrice. Addressing an individual by their proper name fosters a sense of connection and establishes a positive and mutually enriching bond with them.

e. Everyone is vulnerable to unfortunate incidents in life.

Although our thoughts and actions undoubtedly influence many aspects of our lives, it is important to recognize that the course of the world does not always align with our desires. Even divine intervention cannot necessarily bring about alterations to the world in accordance with its desires. Within the context of this narrative, the fly encountered a lamentable circumstance wherein it suffered from a lapse in memory pertaining to its own appellation. Adverse circumstances can occur during the most unforeseeable moments in one's existence. There exists no universally applicable legal provision that precludes the occurrence of such incidents in our case. The Covidpandemic constitutes an instance of calamity that resulted in loss of life, widespread unemployment, and depletion of financial assets for numerous individuals. After a period spanning two complete years, the situation began to return to a state of normalcy. The economy in Sri Lanka experienced a severe downturn that resulted in significant challenges for the population. The main objective is not to imply that life is solely comprised of sorrows and that we should readily accept them. Instead, during periods of adversity, it is advisable to acknowledge one's worries and sadness while simultaneously taking productive measures to address the sorrow and implement remedial measures.

In the face of encountering the deprivation of something of utmost significance in our lives, whether it be an individual dear to us or a job we deeply valued, it is considered conducive to our emotional well-being to experience feelings of sorrow. By casually disregarding the loss without acknowledging its significance, you are essentially attempting to repress a substantial injury with the expectation that it will spontaneously resolve itself. In the occurrences of unpleasant experiences or traumatic events, particularly during one's early years or adolescence, it is common for individuals to exhibit a proclivity towards suppressing or repressing these incidents. These negative past encounters become imprinted within the recesses of the subconscious and can manifest as psychological and psychosomatic ailments during adulthood[5]. In such circumstances, it is imperative to assimilate the encounter, rejuvenate our spirits, and proceed forward with purposeful endeavors.

Step 4:
exploring technology

T
Technology can serve as a valuable asset in eliminating tardiness patterns. Numerous applications are readily accessible that furnish reminders for tasks and deadlines, enabling individuals to maintain organization and adhere to schedules. In addition, certain individuals may provide incentives as a means of motivating individuals to

achieve their objectives or complete tasks within the designated timeframe.

An additional effective method to maintain accountability is by participating in virtual check-ins with colleagues or acquaintances. One may engage in discussions regarding progress, offer encouragement, and ensure mutual accountability in achieving the predetermined objectives.
Regardless of the strategies you choose to employ, it is imperative to bear in mind that overcoming habits of tardiness requires both time and dedication. Persist in your efforts, and in due course, you will successfully cultivate the habit of punctuality.
Step 5:
Developing a Consistent Schedule and Adhering to It

A
Attaining success in effectively addressing tardiness hinges upon

establishing and adhering to a well-defined and consistent schedule. This may entail establishing predetermined schedules for activities such as awakening, grooming, consuming breakfast or lunch, initiating work, and commencing relaxation. It is equally imperative to ensure that these routines are pragmatic and attainable, duly considering external factors like traffic or other obligations.

When dealing with tasks that necessitate completion throughout the day, it is beneficial to decompose them into more manageable stages. This feature facilitates the monitoring of progress and prevents the risk of being overwhelmed by the current task. Additionally, it's important to recognize when you have done something well and reward yourself for reaching a goal or completing an activity on time. By doing this, you can reinforce the notion in your mind that success can be attained through adherence to a consistent regimen.

In conclusion, it is important to adopt a compassionate attitude towards oneself in the event of deviating from the established plan or failing to meet a designated deadline. Identify the factors that contributed to the failure and devise strategies to rectify the situation going forward, such as establishing more attainable objectives or enhancing the existing support infrastructure. Through diligent effort and unwavering commitment, you will swiftly eliminate those tendencies of arriving late permanently.

Fostering Focus

Envision a scenario in which you find yourself immersed in a comfortable and inviting workspace adorned with vibrant hues and motivational quotations adorning the walls. You avail yourself of a brief respite to engage in bodily movements and practice deep inhalation and exhalation, thereby experiencing a newfound sense of revitalization and enthusiasm upon resuming your tasks. Due to the positive atmosphere in your surroundings, you are experiencing a sense of motivation and resolve.

One effective strategy for mitigating distractions involves crafting an environment that is both conducive and inviting. This may entail embellishing your work environment with hues and objects that evoke feelings of joy, such as botanical elements or portraits of cherished individuals. By cultivating a work environment that is conducive to your personal preferences and satisfaction, there is a heightened likelihood that you will be motivated to sustain your focus and accomplish your tasks.

An additional strategy for mitigating distractions involves integrating physical activity and exercise into your daily routine. Engaging in consistent physical activity can effectively mitigate stress levels and enhance concentration, thereby facilitating the management of distractions. Please contemplate engaging in a brief stroll or performing stretching exercises during your allotted breaks throughout the course of your workday. In addition to enhancing your ability to concentrate, this practice will contribute to the enhancement of your overall state of well-being.

It is equally essential to pause periodically and restore mental energy during the course of the day. By allowing for moments of cerebral respite and revitalization, individuals may experience enhanced productivity and an increased capacity to effectively navigate and mitigate potential distractions upon resuming their professional endeavors. This may entail engaging in a brief period of rest, employing techniques of mindfulness, or temporarily removing oneself from work tasks for a few moments.

Similar to a computer system, it is imperative for optimum performance that your brain also requires intermittent periods of rest and rejuvenation. Just as an excessive number of applications running concurrently on a computer can lead to reduced speed and increased memory usage, an overwhelming abundance of thoughts and tasks occupying your mind can likewise impede your productivity and diminish your cognitive capabilities. Engaging in periodic periods of rest and cultivating mindfulness can facilitate the process of cleansing one's thoughts and replenishing one's energy levels. By incorporating these methodologies and approaches into your daily routine, you can enhance your capacity to concentrate and consequently lead a fulfilling and efficacious existence that aligns with your aspirations.

Discern the period of the day when your productivity is at its peak and strategically allocate significant responsibilities during that timeframe.

In the pursuit of enhancing productivity, acquiring knowledge about one's distinctive biological rhythms, commonly referred to as chronotype, presents a notable benefit. Each individual possesses an intrinsic physiological mechanism, commonly referred to as the circadian rhythm, which governs various bodily functions such as the alternating patterns of sleep and wakefulness, hormonal secretions, and even mood variations. The energy levels and cognitive functioning that you exhibit throughout the day are influenced by your chronotype, consequently impacting your level of productivity. Through determining the period during which you are most productive and structuring your schedule accordingly, you can enhance your efficiency and carry out important tasks more effectively.

The notion of a "biological prime time" has been put forth by specialists in productivity, denoting the particular period of the day during which an individual's energy levels, concentration, and emotional state reach their highest point. For the majority of individuals, this occurs during a time frame spanning from 2 to 4 hours. Nevertheless, the duration of this timeframe may vary significantly among individuals. Certain individuals, commonly known as "morning larks," experience enhanced alertness and concentration during the morning hours. Other individuals, commonly referred to as "night owls," attain the pinnacle of their productivity during the evening hours. Additionally, there exists a category of individuals who experience their highest levels of productivity during the early afternoon, commonly referred to as "afternoon individuals."

Determining your biological prime time entails carefully monitoring your energy and concentration levels throughout the duration of the day. One may observe distinct patterns, for instance, experiencing a decline in energy levels after lunch yet subsequently experiencing a resurgence of energy in the late afternoon. One might consider maintaining a succinct journal documenting their energy levels on a hourly basis, or employing productivity applications designed to monitor one's work patterns. As time progresses, a discernible pattern will begin to manifest itself, providing you with a guiding framework to organize and allocate your tasks efficiently.

After determining your most productive period during the day, it is imperative to allocate and safeguard this time exclusively for your critical and demanding endeavors, particularly those that demand the highest cognitive capabilities. Some possible options could involve activities that encompass the resolution of problems, the application of strategic thought, or the demonstration of creative abilities. By synchronizing these tasks with your periods of highest productivity, you can guarantee that you are delivering optimal performance in the most vital facets of your job.

On the contrary, you have the option to arrange tasks that have lower priority or require less effort, such as administrative tasks, meetings, or routine duties, during periods when your energy tends to decrease. By adopting this approach, you are effectively capitalizing on the natural fluctuations in your energy levels throughout the day, rather than engaging in a futile struggle against them.

Furthermore, you may employ tactics to optimize your energy levels and concentration during the periods when you are most productive, in conjunction with synchronizing your work schedule to your internal circadian rhythm. Some alternative expressions in a more formal tone could be: - These could encompass tactics such as reducing disturbances, incorporating brief intervals for rejuvenation, and upholding optimal levels of hydration and nutrition. - Potential approaches could encompass the reduction of distractions, the incorporation of periodic breaks for revitalization, and the adherence to proper hydration and nutrition. - Viable strategies may involve limiting disruptions, incorporating intermittent periods of recuperation, and adhering to appropriate levels of hydration and nutrition.

It should be emphasized that an individual's chronotype has the potential to undergo changes throughout their lifetime, which can be attributed to various factors like aging and modifications in their lifestyle. Hence, it is advantageous to periodically evaluate your most efficient periods and make appropriate adjustments to your timetable.

Furthermore, while the conscientious consideration of one's chronotype and the subsequent organization of tasks based on this knowledge can greatly optimize productivity, it may not always be practicable due to external limitations such as work timetables, familial obligations, or societal conventions. In such instances, it is imperative to explore alternative approaches to effectively regulate one's energy and concentration levels. These may include adhering to a consistent sleep routine, engaging in mindfulness exercises, and periodically taking deliberate pauses.

Conclusively, determining your most efficacious period of the day and organizing significant tasks accordingly can significantly boost productivity. It pertains to the collaboration with the innate rhythms of one's body, as opposed to working in opposition to them. By comprehending and honoringyour individual biological rhythm, you have the potential to enhance your work schedule to achieve utmost efficiency and holistic wellness.

The Fallout From Ineffective Time Management.

Let's also evaluate the consequences of bad time management.

● Bad workflow

The lack of effective planning and adherence to objectives leads to a decrease in overall efficiency. To illustrate, in situations where there are several essential tasks at hand, an efficient approach would involve executing interconnected activities concurrently or sequentially. However, without adequate preparation in advance, there is a possibility that you may encounter the need to frequently switch directions or retrace your steps during the completion of your task. It results in a reduction in overall efficiency and a decline in output quality.

● Wasted time

Insufficient allocation of time results in time being squandered. For instance, when you engage in casual conversations with friends on social media while completing an assignment, you are inadvertently diverting your attention and squandering valuable time.

● Lack of control

Not being aware of the subsequent obligation results in a lack of command over one's life. It has the potential to result in heightened levels of stress and anxiety.

● Substandard execution of work ● Poor craftsmanship ● Inadequate standard of performance ● Low-quality output ● Inferior job execution

Inadequate time management can significantly impede the overall quality of one's work. As a case in point, the need to expedite tasks in the final moments often compromises the standard of outcomes.

● Bad reputation

In the event that clients or your organization are unable to rely upon your consistency in promptly achieving objectives, their expectations and perceptions of you are significantly and detrimentally affected. If a client cannot rely upon your ability to consistently meet deadlines, they are likely to seek alternative business opportunities elsewhere.

● Disappointing Performance

Due to the limited availability of time, effective management of this resource plays a pivotal role in shaping your achievements. Numerous studies have substantiated the claim that individuals who effectively manage their time exhibit higher levels of productivity and achievement compared to those who do not. Individuals who exhibit poor time management skills have a propensity to neglect their responsibilities, exhibiting a lack of self-care, thus compromising their professional efficacy and the overall performance of the organization. To enhance your job performance, it is imperative to effectively allocate your time and prioritize tasks based on their significance.

● Missing Deadlines
There are no surprises in this situation - Inadequate time management can result in a series of challenges pertaining to meeting deadlines. To begin with, you might encounter difficulties in recollecting the impending deadlines or their respective due dates. A lack of comprehension regarding prioritization can also result in failure to meet deadlines. This occurrence is not uncommon when inadequate management of time results in an environment dominated by stress and apprehension.

● Challenging Interpersonal Dynamics and Social Circumstances
The manner in which one handles their time has an impact on their interpersonal connections. During periods of intense busyness, it is often effortless to overlook the importance of maintaining meaningful relationships with the people in our vicinity. To clarify, when we allocate our time and

energy to the daily obligations of life. Numerous individuals allocate insufficient time to spend with their loved ones due to their overwhelming efforts in managing their extensive agenda. Moreover, their lack of sufficient time management skills further exacerbates the situation.

● Stress and Anxiety

There exist multiple factors that contribute to stress and concern. Several factors contribute to these conditions, including mental health disorders as well as sleep deprivation or alterations in their environment. Regardless of the underlying factors, these causes have the potential to impact your ability to effectively manage your time. Nevertheless, the repercussions become apparent when one experiences a deficiency in their time management skills. It consistently engenders concern and apprehension.

Chapter 7 - Mitigating Diversions and Sustaining Concentration

Many individuals struggle with managing their time and maintaining focus due to various sources of diversion. They may manifest in various formats, such as electronic correspondences, notifications through social media platforms, telephonic communications, and several others. Such diversions have the potential to disturb the smooth flow of our work, diminish our overall efficiency, and divert our attention away from the critical tasks at hand. To effectively minimize diversions and maintain concentration, it is crucial to comprehend how distractions adversely affect our productivity and establish tactics for surmounting them.

A significant manner in which distractions impact our productivity is by disrupting our state of flow. Flow refers to a heightened state of cognitive and emotional involvement wherein individuals become fully engrossed and deeply immersed in the task before them. When we are operating in a state of optimal performance, we exhibit heightened levels of productivity, creativity, and concentration. Nevertheless, interruptions can promptly disrupt our productivity and divert our attention away from the current assignment. To maintain an undisturbed state of concentration and enhance productivity, one should prioritize reducing disruptions and devising effective techniques for swiftly regaining a state of optimal focus in the event of interruptions.

An additional manner in which distractions impact our level of productivity is by elevating our stress levels. When subjected to a continuous influx of diversions, individuals may find themselves inundated, thereby attributing to feelings of overwhelm, stress, anxiety, and ultimately, burnout. To ensure the mitigation of distractions and maintenance of concentration, it is crucial to cultivate beneficial strategies for managing stress, such as practicing mindfulness and engaging in meditation. These practices can effectively lower our stress levels and enhance our general state of wellness.

Moreover, apart from comprehending the ramifications of distractions on our efficiency, there exist multiple techniques at our disposal to eradicate interruptions and maintain utmost concentration. A few of these tactics encompass:

● Disable notifications: An highly efficient approach to eliminate distractions involves the deactivation of notifications on all of your devices. By implementing this measure, you will be spared from the incessant influx of notifications, thereby enabling you to concentrate on the current task.

● Employ the use of an application blocker: An alternate method to effectively eradicate distractions involves incorporating the use of an application blocker. This feature will inhibit your access to specific applications during designated periods, enabling you to maintain concentrated attention on the current endeavor.

● Set aside dedicated focus time: Setting aside dedicated focus time each day can help you eliminate distractions and stay focused. Throughout this period, kindly deactivate your notifications, close your email application, and direct your complete attention to the current undertaking.

● Establish an environment devoid of distractions: By establishing an environment free from distractions, you can effectively eliminate disturbances and maintain your concentration. This may encompass tasks such as arranging your work area, decluttering, and limiting the presence of distractions within your immediate surroundings.

● Engage in the cultivation of mindfulness and meditation: The cultivation of mindfulness and meditation can facilitate the elimination of distractions and the maintenance of focused attention by mitigating stress levels and enhancing one's overall state of being.

To summarize, distractions pose a significant challenge for individuals in terms of time management and concentration. To enhance concentration and minimize diversions, it is crucial to comprehend the influence of distractions on our efficacy and formulate approaches to conquer them. Through the act of disabling notifications, utilizing a software tool to block applications, allocating specific time for concentrated work, establishing an environment devoid of distractions, and engaging in mindfulness and meditation exercises, one can effectively eradicate interruptions, maintain concentration, and optimize productivity, thus leading to the attainment of set objectives.

www.ingramcontent.com/pod-product-compliance
Lightning Source LLC
Chambersburg PA
CBHW052144110526
44591CB00012B/1858